The Yearning Life

The Yearning Life

POEMS

REGINA WALTON

PARACLETE PRESS
BREWSTER, MASSACHUSETTS

2016 First Printing

The Yearning Life: Poems

Copyright © 2016 by Regina Walton

ISBN 978-1-61261-863-0

The Paraclete Press name and logo (dove on cross) are trademarks of Paraclete Press, Inc.

Library of Congress Cataloging-in-Publication Data
Names: Walton, Regina, author.
Title: The yearning life : poems / Regina Walton.
Description: Brewster MA : Paraclete Press Inc., 2016.
Identifiers: LCCN 2016031369 | ISBN 9781612618630 (trade paper)
Subjects: LCSH: Spirituality--Poetry. | Religious poetry, American.
Classification: LCC PS3623.A4548 A6 2016 | DDC 811/.6--dc23
LC record available at https://lccn.loc.gov/2016031369

10 9 8 7 6 5 4 3 2 1

Published by Paraclete Press
Brewster, Massachusetts
www.paracletepress.com

Printed in the United States of America

for Chris

. . . so God, by deferring our hope, stretches our desire; by the desiring, stretches the mind; by stretching, makes it more capacious. Let us desire therefore, my brethren, for we shall be filled. This is our life, that by longing we should be exercised.

—Augustine of Hippo (354–430),
Homily 4 on the First Epistle of John

Thus one creates a readiness and a disposition for receiving the inward, yearning life. When the vessel is ready, noble liquor is poured into it. There is no vessel more noble than the loving soul, nor drink more beneficial than the grace of God.

—Jan van Ruusbroec (1293–1381),
The Spiritual Espousals

Contents

VISITATIONS • 47

SEVEN O'S: ANTIPHONS • 63

SPIRIT and MARROW

EXEMPLUM

A fly lands
On my open book,
And rubs its fingerless palms together
Over the word *askesis*.

Thank you, little black-robed fly,
For showing me
How to be an ascetic.

You see everything,
But own nothing.

To you, no difference
Between paradise and dung,
The father's banquet and the pigsty.

And every still moment finds you
Ceaselessly caressing
Invisible beads.

THE MIRACULOUS CATCH OF FISH
Luke 5:1–11

What led them all, shimmering net of a mind,
To pivot their arrowhead bodies
In startled unison
Toward the boat's empty underbelly,
The flaccid snare submerged?

What glint was caught
By each lidless eye
Compelling them *en masse*—
Their sleek iridescence pressed together,
Longing to be drawn up?

How did the striated sun look,
Wave-woven on the water's surface,
As they beheld it breathlessly from above—
Suffocating object lesson
Of abundant life?

THE SLOUGH

I left my skin in a pile on the floor.
The fresh one was moist, and downy
And smelled of milk.

The old wrinkled heap with face full of holes,
Wig-like scalp and empty fingers,
Already grayish, settling into its creases,
Could be gathered up,
Arms and legs tucked
Into the rounded pouch of the buttocks
And delicately folded along the belly's long tear,
Caesarean of myself.

How many papery layers in our composition?
Pulse and breath, spongy organs, muscle-wrapped bone
Sealed in a translucent envelope,
A marvel of packaging.

Still, what relief every few years to step out,
To stretch and reach newly elastic, unlined,
To yawn that first unbounded yawn again.

THE CHARLES RIVER CHANNEL

Someone has fixed a camera on a ledge
To spy on the river
So at any hour from the TV set in your sterile room
You can watch the glint off the water,
Rowers slicing through current
With mechanical arms.

The sound is linked to Harvard Radio,
Usually classical, but on Sunday
A program called "Blues Hangover."
This is the best time, early on the Lord's Day,
Whiskey voices laid over the river's calm,
Only one or two runners on the path,
A few Subarus on Memorial Drive.

Sit up carefully
In your backless shroud for the living
With the white blanket across your lap,
And watch the Charles River Channel.

It's like a little of the next life in this one,
Or another life set next to yours,
Emptied of past and future,
That for a few moments you can enter.

Morning light that odd mixture of bright and dim,
As the quiet waters
Head into Boston to meet the tides.

SPIRIT AND MARROW

So thickly knotted,
The holy twins—
Real and ghost,
Untold apart.

Like the question:
Did the first body rise
From the earth or the sea?
And was it more or less than us?

Captured span
Without measure,
Volumes bound
And sealed in dust.

So thickly knotted,
Only the word splits through.

AUTOBIOGRAPHICAL POEM

I started out small
And got smaller.
Loved, humiliated, self-enclosed.

Some days lifting up my hands,
Others carrying my cross
Where shoulders meet spine.

I was knit together,
And now I've knit someone else
Thoughtlessly.

Not that it happened without a thought,
But surely
It wasn't the thoughts that did it.

I bled out when he arrived,
So they filled me back up
With the blood of another.

Now I am the same
By half.
Thank You.

EACH OF US

The steady limitedness of each of us,
Each step, breath, grasp, swallow—
Each of us a miracle of finitude.

Animated aggregates, sewn up with invisible thread,
Ruled by the gentle tyranny of the subjunctive:
What could happen, what might, what we would do—

As our cells discard and recreate themselves,
Continual germination and decay of
Each little fiefdom of longing.

SONG OF SONGS

I visited a woman, ninety-one,
With a Bible and a biography of Pascal

By her bed,
And she said:

I was looking for that word
In the Song of Songs—it means Beautiful—

Comely?
Yes—'I am black but I am comely.'

And her eyes shone clear
As she lay back and smiled.

THE HEART TREMBLES IN ITS NEST OF BONE

Inside the laboring chambers,
Rhythm given,
Restless on purpose,
The underlying dotted line—
Expectation expounding.

Quickening liquid
Spasmed and sorted,
Wrangled in ventricles
Our veined ocean—
Each pulse waving us on,
Waving us on.

THE LORD ENCLOSED THE SEA

Then enclosed some of the sea in us—
And so we crave to taste
More of what we are,
Visceral abyss.

To taste but not to drink—
Parched inversion of drowning, unslaking
But to place a few grains on the tongue,

Animal, mineral,
Salt marsh of the body,
Fermenting memory—

Until the sea-wind reclaims its kin,
Ebb and flow freed from its hold,
Sweeping us back in.

FIRST DAY

The baby: hale and pink and strong and fine.
But beached and bleached, you are much less sanguine
And so, two pints of blood by plastic line
Leach their slow way into your opened vein.
The scarlet bags like lungs suspended from
The scarecrow pole, unwanted hanger-on
This trinity: child, mater, sire gone
To sleep in a hard chair.
                              Now the bald sum
Of all your pains naps in a plastic bin.
Your web of tubes a tether to the bed;
The buzzing, ringing, beeping, healing din.
Who thought, on your first day, who expected
So soon, to find so much of yourself gone?
In time, you will get used to being wrong.

STYLUS

Leaning back with a pencil,
Crossing out, filling in.
Quiet house, empty mug
Against a muted blue glaze of light.

Shadow of my human hand on paper,
So calm in its gentle, incremental
Passing away.

The privilege of holding a pencil—
Light embrace, circumscribed choreography,
As the tangled boughs sway and sigh into winter.

BORROWED BACK

Like metal shavings to a magnet,
The weight of the body aggregates,
And is dispersed.

What is given, and what is withdrawn?
What is pulled together and apart?

Drawn—compelled by a force, or surfacing as a line.
Drawn towards, and drawn as.
Captivated, and constituted.

The figure itself, and the lines of the figure.
The ink as it dries.

Lent by the mystery, and borrowed back.

SHOWINGS

SLEIGHT

Before it was a card trick, a disappeared
Quarter reborn from unsuspecting ear,
Sleight meant skill—
Not the magician's sticky fingers but
The steady hand of the archer
Bracing, drawing, releasing
The slender body with its
Barbed tongue, killing shank,
Its fletching, man-made wing
In measured flight, gentle arc reenacting
The intimacy of bow and arrow—
How the bow, over years,
Bends towards the string, spine
Curved in to its beloved,
Loosed and lost, again and again—
Sometimes retrieved unbroke and bloody,
Sometimes settling in the forest's gullet.
The practice of sighting right—
Dexterous harmony of tensions,
Silent music of the hand and eye.
True aim, water-clear, the pulse of it,
Distance encapsuled, speed matching speed.
But the years are freighted with human suspicion:
Craft turns crafty, art sours
To artifice, tricks and cleverness,
To beguiled applause instead of
A shaft through the heart.

LOOKING AT MEMLING

Today he does not want to read *The Runaway Bunny*
Or *Blueberries for Sal*, but drags over
The heavy art book with the sloe-eyed
Angel on the cover.
He sits in my lap as we flip past
Three-quarter profiles of men with pageboys and embroidered
    collars
Until we arrive at the mother lode—
Painting after painting of the Madonna and Child.

He is delighted that Jesus, like him, is strawberry-blond
And round-bellied, leaning in to nurse
From a pale, grapefruit-sized orb
Protruding from the yards and yards
Of the BVM's drapery.
But the proportions are off—the long-awaited one
Is neither baby nor child,
More like a homunculus, who could,
After suckling, raise an elfin finger
And start sorting sheep from goats then and there.
Mary, amid her shining tresses and upholstery,
Wears the same languid expression in each pose.

We pause at one picture
With a dollhouse castle in the corner.
He asks if Jesus will go inside it.
Yes, I say, and suddenly I imagine
The Mother of God snapping awake and climbing off her throne,
Dragging her voluminous folds behind her,
Turning while she still can—
Pulling away from the gaggle of prophets,
Scaling the slope towards the shelter
With the babe on her hip,
Around her neck his tiny, unmarked hands.

THE YEARNING LIFE

Wax tablet and stylus in hand beneath the trees,
The hermit priest van Ruusbroec
Parsed the soul's progress into thirds:
Lives Active, Contemplative, and

Between them, the Yearning Life,
Where you rest in constant restlessness
Having made a decent start, but not yet
Streaming from abandoned self
Into the heart of light.

For a created vessel
Cannot contain an uncreated good;
That is why there is an eternal
Hungry avidity here.

Each holy favor, eagerly awaited, consumed,
Only melts into more craving.

And satiety is the missing dish.

THE HAND-CLASP

I'm sorry for always dragging you to various shrines
On our vacations, shrines or monasteries or churches or
The remnant of any place where a small
Band of eccentrics once dedicated themselves to God.

Climbing a million stairs in Montreal with those
Casting about for a miracle (an elevator for the infirm);
The abbey in Oregon with the senile and fiercely-wimpled nun
Who forced us to take four copies of each pamphlet;
The convent museum in Quebec City with exhibits of handiwork
     of the sisters
Who sewed vestments until they were blind or arthritically
     crippled;
The round barn built by egalitarian celibates in Massachusetts;
Or drinking powdered coffee in France
With thousands of university students camped out to sit
On the floor and sing chants with men in white.

I've never believed with Eliot
That in some places "prayer has been valid,"
With the implication that in others, not
(Though we've been to Little Gidding, too,
Wandering around the small graveyard to the *pop pop* of
     pheasant hunting)—
Prayer is valid in all places—
And yet I keep pulling you around, don't I,
To wherever holy fools have set up shop.

But it's not validity I'm after,
It is expectation—
To recover a few calcified droplets of the longing
That once flowed like sap,
To witness whatever I can
Of the believing life manifest:
The concentrated playing out
Of hope in resurrection, specific or general—

The daily fumbling reach into darkness,
The wavering but renewable certainty
Of a hand-clasp
On the other side.

SEMEIA

Before we could interpret,
We knew the world as full of signs—
That one points to another,
Each nests in each
All the way down to
The pulsing kernel
Of the sparrow's heart.

How could we know at the start
Their everlastingness?
Continuing on while we disintegrate—
Even scratches on the page outlast us,
Oak to grass. Humiliating.

Inscrutable beauty of the characters—
Sing the lists of letters again
And perhaps they will arrange themselves
Into a correspondence—
Hebrew to Greek, Greek to Hebrew,
The revelation always
Re-revealed.

Translation's aftermath
The proliferation of signs.
Escaping their alchemists,
Burning like constellations,
Reading us back.

RAKE'S REGRESS

Slow fever
Spreading down the tree
Signals the incessant buzz
Of man and his machine.

Banshee-cries of conjured wind
Blasting the green patches
Of our city,
Shrieking to each other
Over fence and hedge
With poisoned breath.

I watch my neighbor from my desk—
Friend, consider
The quiet simplicity of the rake,
Its supple wooden pole
And peacock-spray of tines,
The pleasant rustle of leaves across earth
And honest muscle-work.

Consider the Japanese tea masters
And their teaching:
Stray leaves make the lawn more beautiful.
But goggled and earmuffed,
He is lost, I see,
In cacophonic
Reverie.

INVENTION

Design slips to drawn,
Idea to actual.
Realized: not awareness but accomplishment.
Then the all starts to lack—
Here little flaws burrow up like insects
Hatched from soil,
There a whole limb
Goes missing.
Thought cut off so thing can live—
But neither is perfected.
Perfection, that doorless circle,
Enclosed garden of splintered glimpses.

INTERVAL

Inter-being, bridge of between
Natural rest, handbreadth space in the wall

Tacit resignation from the world of tasks
Erasure of generative moments

Responding to none, the chord in waves
Value-neutral, *apatheia*, like the old
Abbas in their desert-dwellings.

Leave well enough alone;
In fact, leave all.

THE NEEDLE

My

Track is front

And back.   Limbless,

All-   Purpose.

Agility   And

Ability   To bind

And   Unwind.

I am unfeeling,

But bring

Healing.

To thread

My head,

You

Must

Align

your

eye

with

m

i

n

e

.

NY|NJ

A tile in the Lincoln Tunnel: squint
Your eyes and pay attention from your high
Seat on the bus bench for the whole ride through,
And you will see it for an instant, lit
By tiny lines of lanterns, glowing white
Above the untrod sidewalk that we'd use
If we were stranded underground, under
Water, crossing over.
                              Icon like the
Whale suspended, life-sized, breathless, hung by
Cables in the cavernous museum,
NY|NJ: *oikoumene*, earliest
Boundary, like the whale's eye, witness to ceaseless
Tides of humans, carnal motion,
Still point fixed in unseen ocean.

SHELTERED CIRCLE

Rusted fence in a swath of sun,
Linked diamonds lit,

Diagonal nobility of the tessellations
Entwined against the wind.

Plume-mimic of the squirrel's tail
Spirals up a tree.

A red spot on a black wing,
Fir needles spread in a sheltered circle.

As much as anyone can have of anything,
As much or more.

MY EDUCATION

I think I am somewhere between
Set free and ruined.

I keep strange company.
Those who professed to me
Found foundations unfashionable;
So now I dig the basement,
Having built the house.

The best were early:
One woman taught us a song in Swahili
About making sandals from old tires.
Another had me recite
From the King James Bible for prizes.
And every year into the city to pay homage
To dinosaur relics,
Or out to the woods where green-hatted men
Showed us how trees bleed syrup.

All the books I taught myself,
Excavating and insulating.

And it has kept going on and on.
I could never just throw my cap
In the air and leave.

I cannot tell anymore
What I expect to find.
But I will know it when I see it—
I will trade all that I have.

WOODEN SPOON

Little oar paddling across thousands of family meals,
Worn and scorched,
Weathered velvet-soft like an antler.

Pots and pans, bowls, utensils, kettles:
All modernized and polymerized,
Lab-tested and innovated upon.

But the long-handled spoon the baby
Gnaws, amid a plastic menagerie on the floor,
Could appear in a prairie diorama,
Totemic artifact of the kitchen.

Little hearth god overseeing
The good outcome of all domestic undertakings,
Presiding at the stove, over
Alchemy of olive oil and onions.
Do not invoke its wrath—
The threat in childhood of a
Stinging rebuke on our behinds.

Wooden spoon in my grandmother's casket,
A lifetime of stirring, folding, frying, mixing, skimming
Now concluded—
But braced for the life to come,
Ready to help serve up that heavenly banquet.

HAPPY ACCIDENT (I)

What was it called—the Fortunate
Fall. But we didn't fall,
We were pushed.

Was it a set-up,
All the way up?

The serpent
Has no comment, now.

But the rip in the fabric
Was the hole
He fell through,

Our fortune falling
Into boundedness,
Into a body,
Falling out of a womb,
Caught by what hands.

HAPPY ACCIDENT (II)

Sublime pleasure of smacking a hard-boiled egg—
Watch the delicate fissures crevice out.

The first strategic pick:
Tiny chip under fingernail, or
Long unspooling of cracked porcelain?

Glued with translucent skin,
Domed firmament.
On the whole, the perfect broken thing

Ideal form to gospel fragments,
Discarded shards of genesis.

POEM ACCOMPANYING AN ALLERGEN-FREE BIRTHDAY DESSERT

You can't eat flour, sugar, or milk
You can't eat yarn, pebbles, or footprints

Every blade of grass outside
Has another blade of grass somewhere in the world
It could live with forever

I baked you this custard using the *via negativa*
I substituted the Cloud of Unknowing for milk

I substituted this day with another day
That kissed you with the pink inside of a shell,
That held you in its fist,

Next to the opal fingernails of Jupiter's moons,
Above the inscrutable speech of airplanes.

VISITATIONS

PSALM 131

My grandma put her breasts in a drawer
And that was that—
The prosthetics, anyway, meant to fill her bra,
The originals claimed by cancer in my childhood.

For all her children, her breasts had never suckled—
The doctors put her under her before each birth,
Then told her
Nursing was for savages.

Ann, after the Virgin's mother,
She prayed out loud and often to her own.

On the feast of the Annunciation,
Five years gone, she visited me
And in that no-place dream space,
Our bosom-embrace renewed, I felt them—

Hesed, womb-love that moved over the abyss,
That mothered the churning darkness into life—
Her wholeness shocked me awake.

MIDNIGHT BUS FROM NEW YORK CITY
WITH THOMAS TRAHERNE

Everyone settles back
To their glowing devices.

No one else cares about
The arrangement of lights across New Jersey,
This museum exhibit of the day's zero
Slowly fogging with collective breath.

The hum and rumble of the bus
Overlaid on the mind's machinations,
Smoothing them, like the night smooths
This strange pastoral:
Meadowlands of empty parking lots
Beyond the highway-side grasses, tall and swaying,

As each streetlight grows arm-beams,
Reaching to one another—
Across ramps and bridges,
The rolling darkness, out to where
Someone sleeps the deep sleep of a child.

THE RICH YOUNG MAN
Mark 10:17–25

They had been such a holy bargain,
The poor: I could give liberally
And receive their clasped hands
And bows in the street
And have plenty, more than plenty,
To live on still, feasting and filling my house at my pleasure.

Was I restless in this life,
Or did I simply seek confirmation
That I would really drink the water
This man claimed to have dowsed?

I could tell, when we spoke,
That the rabbi wanted to collect me,
That I could lend a silver sheen
To his wayfaring band of
Fisherman and unattended women.
And he said I lacked only one thing.

But the requirement
Unraveled all my satisfaction,
Soured my contentment—
In front of everyone
He showed my open hand to be clenched closed,
My courtyards a prison.
How could I give it all away
And join him,

To sleep and eat at the hands of strangers?
I left the crowd with a poisoned stream in my blood
And he did not call after me.

I heard of his naked disgrace,
And his followers hunted down.
I heard too the rumors
That he walked in white through walls
And broke bread with his broken hands.
And once or twice in the early hours
Roaming the streets, I heard those he left behind,
Singing from a second floor.

I never joined them.
But I never married,
And year by year I have chipped away
At the birthright that held me in its fist,
Ridding myself of it in secret,
Clipping the cords one by one.
No one salutes me in the street now, shabby old man.
My room is cold.

But on the last day I will face him,
And see what this treasure-cask he spoke of
Holds.

ON THE FEAST OF
BERNARD OF CLAIRVAUX

Between the Artichoke and Merrimack,
Their streams converging to a salty kiss,
I sit and watch a lone goldfinch drop down
Onto a thistle, tearing at its head.
This bird, once captured by Italian masters
And painted in the infinite infant grip
Of Christ, now freely plucks at seed and throws
Down milky threads like chaff in meadow grass.

Doctor Mellifluous, not honey-tongued
But named after the labor of extraction
Of golden wisdom hidden in the comb:
Golden in your age, insatiable,
Held in the vise-grip of the Bridegroom come,
You tore away at heaven until it opened.

STUDENT TEACHER

The Student Teacher stands
Behind her massive desk.
The bell has rung,
Shoes, backpacks, arms, voices
Have scuffled and pitched themselves outwards.

It is that sacred crevice of time,
Handbreadth space between School and No-School
Like *sandhya*, the joints of the day,
When Hindu sannyasis pray in purple light.

She is the Student Teacher,
A name
Which cancels itself out.

She has taken a vow
Never to raise her voice;
She abstains from the faculty pastime
Of slandering the young.

She strives to treat all with equity
In matters involving the raising of hands,
The scrawling of signatures,
The flecking of manuscripts.

And so she often stands alone
Like this,
Chalked palms together
For just a few moments
Before letting herself out the heavy side door,

Past the raucous line of saffron buses to the gray one on the
    corner
Full of silent adults, idling, then
Lurching towards the river.

ALEX

Driving through Central Square I thought
I saw him in front of the YMCA,
Though I had been to his funeral
Years ago now,
At the church next door,
Which was where he died, in the basement

In the arms of *Mater Ecclesia*
In a leftover rummage sale armchair,
Where the priest found him
With a cup of juice on the table
That he had sipped,
Leaning back
To sigh out his breath.

The service leaflet startling
With its picture of him moon-faced,
Maybe just in his twenties,
Looking at the world from a staircase.
The next thirty years a spiral of wasting,
From the wasting disease of this age.

He was the longest-lived with it, he said,
Medically documented: he wore this
Like an award,
His ticket to that corner of heaven reserved
For the utterly unyielding.

Icon of prayer in my memory—
Hollow cheeks and upturned palms,
Standing stooped in the aisle of the chapel,
His petitions loud, echoing,
For those with AIDS and cancer; for healing without cure.
Tote bag of paper scraps at his feet,
Names and numbers, constellation of friends, agencies,
Weak net that we were.

After the service I helped an old monk
Inch across Mass Ave.,
Holding his arm and his hand
Still cool in his robes,
Despite the force of heat all around us.

HOMECOMING SUNDAY

Children arch their backs against the pews,
Men catalogue pocket change.
Gold earrings catch the light,
Sparkle off the walls,

Distracting the minister as he greets
An elderly woman with lacquered curls.
Her hand caught in his, she notices
How his nose resembles a modest beak.

The organ swoops down on the opening hymn.
His shoes pinch down the aisle.
Smoothing his stole, turning to face
His flock, the minister
Inhales,

Ruffles out his neck
And spreads his tail feathers—
Brown-gray, shimmering with purple—
Spanning the Communion table.

Later some will say
He fanned them like a peacock; others
Compare it to the dignified disclosure
Of a wild turkey.

After the service they watch him
Wing away over the low hills,
Wistful and relieved.

ENOCH'S WIFE

> Enoch walked with God; then he was no more,
> because God took him.
>> —*Genesis 5:24*

I wish I'd never said
If you love God so much,
why don't you go
and live with Him instead.

AULD LANG SYNE

I can only wish you happy new year
By lighting a candle.
My friend, you are ashes.

That last first night
We had to keep it so dark
For your eyes, your head.

The shrimp was a bad idea,
Little bowls of nothing
But their broken tails.

The television's frantic halo,
The three of us sitting around you
On the mattress with our drinks,
Sandbagging you in.

How you twisted
The wire cap
Of the champagne bottle
Into a little chair,

So gently,
With your dying hands.

NEWMAN'S REMAINS

They exhumed him, the great Cardinal—
He deserved a transfer
Behind the altar from this muddy plot,
Transparent veneration
Fitting his elevation.

And also, let it be said,
To separate him from his beloved,
Another priest, in whose grave
It was his wish to be buried.
And they had rested peacefully together
These hundred and twenty years.
Such an attachment
Unseemly for a saint,
Even in death.

But when they opened the coffin,
Not even a relic—
His latest miracle
To have translated himself
Into dust, disintegration complete
With the first rush of air.

Nothing to disturb,
They sealed the grave again.
At the last, as the poet said
Of another tomb,
What will survive of us is love.

SEVEN O'S: ANTIPHONS

THE "GREAT O ANTIPHONS" are short verses chanted before and after the *Magnificat* (Song of Mary) in the monastic evening office of Vespers, one a day, from December 17 through December 23 in the liturgical season of Advent, the period of preparation and repentance before Christmas. They entered Christian worship before the ninth century, and have their source in the prophetic books of the Hebrew Scriptures. The hymn "O Come, O Come Emmanuel" is a nineteenth-century translation and compilation of these antiphons. The Latin text of the antiphons is from the *Breviarium Romanorum*, 1870 edition. The English translation is modernized from *The English Hymnal*.

I

O Sapientia, quae ex ore Altissimi prodisti,
attingens a fine usque ad finem fortiter, suaviter
disponensque omnia: veni ad docendum nos
viam prudentiae.

*O Wisdom, which came out of the mouth of the
Most High, and reaches from one end to the other,
mightily and sweetly ordering all things: Come
and teach us the way of prudence.*

O SAPIENTIA

Holy souls bear your emblem:
The serpent and the dove entwined.
First fashioner—always proceeding, never arriving,
Three-winged flight always circling.

Spotless mirror of divinity—polished clear
To invisibility. We wait for corrosion
To show your face, the outline of your lack.
Many claim your quicksilver substance,
But you do not so much give a mantle as
Land lightly before moving on.

Stretched from one end to the other, you are strained thin
Like beaten gold—best in layers, applied at a cost.
Come Sophia, like the bird of prey you are—
Swoop down on your imitators; put things right.

II

O Adonai, et dux domus Israel, qui Moysi in
igne flammae rubi apparuisti, et ei in Sina legem
dedisti: veni ad redimendum nos in brachio
extento.

O Adonai and Leader of the house of Israel, who
appeared in the bush to Moses in a flame of fire,
and gave him the Law in Sinai: Come and deliver
us with an outstretched arm.

O ADONAI

Shield against the name given of fire—
Beyond comprehension or captivity,
The use and power of names.
Adonai—what we call you because
The truth of redemption weighs heavily on us—
The smoking mountain, the plagues, the sea's retraction,
Cloud and pillar, bread-speckled desert,
Land of milk and honey and the taste of blood—
All this your Name contains,
Spoken and unspoken at once.

Base of creation, vessel of remembrance
For a hundred billion lost tongues,
I AM, so we are
Momentary embers.

But *Adonai*, you privilege your clay:
You appeared once in a thicket of scrub-brush aflame—
You gave the Way so our burning
Would not consume us—
Come and deliver us again
Into your wilderness.

III

O Radix Jesse, qui stas in signum populorum,
super quem continebunt reges os suum, quem
gentes deprecabuntur; veni ad liberandum nos,
iam noli tardere.

*O Root of Jesse, which stands for an ensign of the
people, at whom kings shall shut their mouths, to
whom the Gentiles shall seek: Come and deliver
us, and tarry not.*

O RADIX JESSE

For still the vision awaits its time.
Creator-native,
Shoot from the clean cut, fullness unfolding.

The root mirrors the branch,
Stone and soil, cloud and wind.
The root mirrors the branch, but must work in darkness:
Myriad tongues dowsing,
Gnarled fingers weaving earth into its net inch by inch,
Growth measured in sky.

Grafted onto Jordan's banks,
Frail shoot nailed to rood, your blood watered the purloined soil.
Remnant of remnant laid in the earth, *Adam-ah*.

But the root knows waiting.
It clings to the rock and won't be torn free,
Web of invisible relations holds it firm.
The root knows death's pretense,
Evades in smallest increments.

No magic but the gathered pulse of Sheol
Awakened to quicken again
Its broken seed.
No magic that the dead rood blossomed—
It is the way of roots.
Root of Jesse, sign of signs—
Come again and fountain the desert.

IV

O Clavis David, et sceptrum domus Israel:
qui aperis, et nemo claudit; claudis, et nemo
aperit: veni et educ vinctum de domo carceris,
sedentem in tenebris, et umbra mortis.

O Key of David, and Scepter of the house of Israel;
that opens and no one shuts, and shuts, and no
one opens: Come and bring the prisoner out of the
prison-house, that sits in darkness and the shadow
of death.

O CLAVIS DAVID

After the blade drained his side
And his body was unhooked from the Cross
And swaddled again and laid back in the cave,
Our Lord turned himself into a key.

Like a harrow broke up the earth,
And himself unlocked the door to Sheol.
He grabbed those ancient hands,
The first ever to clasp, to caress, to strike,
And by the wrists he pulled them out—
This is the story handed down.

Skeleton key,
Glint in gloom,
Its lock-twist chains falling away.
But there are reasons not to open a door,
Many reasons why locks are fashioned.

Those who believe, believe God sees in the dark.
Come Key of David: come harrowing and unbinding—
Rout out from the hidden, traceless places
Every truth entombed.

V

O Oriens, splendor lucis aeternae, et sol justitiae:
veni, et illumina sedentis in tenebris, et umbra
mortis.

O Day-Spring, Brightness of Light everlasting, and
Sun of Righteousness: Come and enlighten him
that sits in darkness and the shadow of death.

O ORIENS

First-fashioned creature, gleaned from darkness:
All was deep-churning murk like a flood, pitch-thick,
Then out of it something leaned—
Less than presence, but gathering itself
Like mists off a lake,
Ghost-formed orb faintly smoldering,
Hands-breadth across.
From this beginning was darkness cleaved.

Dayspring—you sweep yourself up
From horizon's cusp
And run your course like a tireless champion
While all beneath you weary and falter, are swept away or
    renewed.
You are Regeneration; yours is the day
Of the vacant cave.
Come morning star, dawn of our mending,
Our grafting back,
Seed us with your light—
The tip of your flame enough
To ravish away our dross.

VI

O Rex gentium, et desideratus earum, lapisque
angularis, qui facis utraque unum: veni, et salva
hominem, quem de limo formasti.

O King of the nations, and their Desire; the
Cornerstone who makes both one: Come and save
humankind, whom you formed of clay.

O REX GENTIUM

I have set my King on Zion, my holy hill
And there he writhes and bleeds,
And his heart cleaves itself open and is torn away.

You preached the kingdom,
But the kingship you saw for what it was.
King of the forked-tongued crowds,
King of humiliation, lineage of whores,
Birthright of stable muck.
No wonder you said
Your kingdom was elsewhere.

But the astrologers charted you:
At your appearance they packed their instruments
And set off for western wilderness.
You drew them to yourself across the desert,
Cold star shining an apocalypse.
And finding you, could they tell
The weight you would bear,
Cornerstone crushed by what you held together?
Was anyone watching your star
When it bled across the sky, and burst
Into a universe?
Come King of the Nations: return to your seditious faithful,
Cement your fractured people.
Bind us, broken king.

VII

O Emmanuel, Rex et legifer noster, expectatio
gentium, et Salvator earum: veni ad salvandum
nos, Domine Deus noster.

*O Emmanuel, our King and Lawgiver, the Desire
of all nations, and their Salvation: Come and save
us, O Lord our God.*

O EMMANUEL

You came to put on the yoke
Of perishing,
To live under the hourglass dome,
To be the choking bone
In Death's throat.

Translated to flesh,
Spoken into human.
What is it to dwell, Emmanuel?
Mostly longing on both sides.

You gave away immortality
At cost, wrung from your pores,
Sinews stretched
From one end to the other.
You embraced to the point of breaking,
Embraced away yourself,
Lost on myriad hungry mouths.

Come Emmanuel: you who ate and wept and walked,
You who spat and healed.
You who chose, who spoke in figures,
Who slipped away.
You who lay down and got up.
Given, you cannot be unspoken.

ACKNOWLEDGMENTS

Grateful acknowledgment is made to the following publications, in which these poems first appeared:

Anglican Theological Review: Midnight Bus from New York City with Thomas Traherne

ARTS: The Arts in Religious & Theological Studies: The Lord Enclosed the Sea

Asheville Poetry Review: Autobiographical Poem; Student Teacher

Hanging Loose: Poem Accompanying an Allergen-Free Birthday Dessert

Poetry East: Sleight

qarrtsiluni: Homecoming Sunday

Scintilla: Exemplum; On the Feast of Bernard of Clairvaux; Looking at Memling

Soundings East: The Slough

Spiritus: The Yearning Life

Announcing

THE FIRST WINNER
OF THE
"PHYLLIS TICKLE PRIZE IN POETRY"

Paraclete Press is pleased to announce the first winner of the
Phyllis Tickle Prize in Poetry, which honors our longtime friend,
advisor, and member of Paraclete's editorial board.

This prize will be given every other year to a poet unpublished in
volume form. Regina Walton was selected for this award
for this volume, *The Yearning Life*.

About Paraclete Press

Who We Are

Paraclete Press is a publisher of books, recordings, and DVDs on Christian spirituality. Our publishing represents a full expression of Christian belief and practice—from Catholic to Evangelical, from Protestant to Orthodox.

We are the publishing arm of the Community of Jesus, an ecumenical monastic community in the Benedictine tradition. As such, we are uniquely positioned in the marketplace without connection to a large corporation and with informal relationships to many branches and denominations of faith.

What We Are Doing

PARACLETE PRESS BOOKS | Paraclete publishes books that show the richness and depth of what it means to be Christian. Although Benedictine spirituality is at the heart of who we are and all that we do, we publish books that reflect the Christian experience across many cultures, time periods, and houses of worship. We publish books that nourish the vibrant life of the church and its people.

We have several different series, including the best-selling Paraclete Essentials and Paraclete Giants series of classic texts in contemporary English; Voices from the Monastery—men and women monastics writing about living a spiritual life today; our award-winning Paraclete Poetry series as well as the Mount Tabor Books on the arts; best-selling gift books for children on the occasions of baptism and first communion; and the Active Prayer Series that brings creativity and liveliness to any life of prayer.

MOUNT TABOR BOOKS | Paraclete's newest series, Mount Tabor Books, focuses on the arts and literature as well as liturgical worship and spirituality, and was created in conjunction with the Mount Tabor Ecumenical Centre for Art and Spirituality in Barga, Italy.

PARACLETE RECORDINGS | From Gregorian chant to contemporary American choral works, our recordings celebrate the best of sacred choral music composed through the centuries that create a space for heaven and earth to intersect. Paraclete Recordings is the record label representing the internationally acclaimed choir Gloriæ Dei Cantores, praised for their "rapt and fathomless spiritual intensity" by *American Record Guide*; the Gloriæ Dei Cantores Schola, specializing in the study and performance of Gregorian chant; and the other instrumental artists of the Gloriæ Dei Artes Foundation.

Paraclete Press is also privileged to be the exclusive North American distributor of the recordings of the Monastic Choir of St. Peter's Abbey in Solesmes, France, long considered to be a leading authority on Gregorian chant.

PARACLETE VIDEO | Our DVDs offer spiritual help, healing, and biblical guidance for a broad range of life issues including grief and loss, marriage, forgiveness, facing death, bullying, addictions, Alzheimer's, and spiritual formation.

Learn more about us at our website: www.paracletepress.com or phone us toll-free at 1.800.451.5006

SCAN TO READ MORE

MORE PARACLETE POETRY

Slow Pilgrim   The Collected Poems of Scott Cairns
SCOTT CAIRNS

ISBN: 978-1-61261-657-5 • $39.99 French Flaps, Paperback

Scott Cairns has gathered every poem he's ever published in book
form, and has also added previously uncollected work spanning three
decades. A careful introduction by Gregory Wolfe and a tribute preface
by Richard Howard make this the ultimate collection of Cairns's work.

"Among American poets of religious belief at the present time, none is
more skillful, authentic, or convincing than Scott Cairns."
—B. H. Fairchild, poet, national Critics Circle Award winner

"With Dostoyevsky and the psalmists as his traveling companions,
Cairns pursues his peregrinations through frustration and pleasure,
desolation and eros, step by step realizing 'how / fraught, how laden the
visible is.' " **—Kimberly Johnson, poet, author of *A Metaphorical God***

Slow Pilgrim was named Englewood's Best Poetry Book of the year in
2015 for the life and flourishing of the Church.

Prayers of a Young Poet

RAINER MARIA RILKE

ISBN: 978-1-61261-641-4 • $16.00, Paperback

"A powerful alchemy of the heart." — **Bill Moyers, journalist and political commentator**

"This extraordinary early-draft form of some of Rilke's most famous somehow evokes, for me, Leonardo da Vinci's notebooks—it shows the same mix of surety, roughness, genius, and the sense of precipitous creative speed. Rilke's poetry always reminds us what a direct pondering of intimacy and depth might look like. I am most grateful for these muscular translations and Mark Burrows' extended introductory comments...." —**Jane Hirshfield, poet and translator; author most recently of _Ten Windows: How Great Poems Transform the World_**

"In these startling poems brought to us in Mark Burrows' lucid translation, metaphor gives way to metaphor, as each verbal foray into the divine courts a mystery that can be approached but neither comprehended nor defined." —**Peter S. Hawkins, Professor of Religion and Literature, Yale Divinity School**

Available from most booksellers or through Paraclete Press: www.paracletepress.com; 1-800-451-5006